The Key Facts™ on Chile

Chile

Essential Information on Chile

By Patrick W. Nee

The Internationalist®
www.internationalist.com

The Internationalist®

International Business, Investment, and Travel

Published by:

The Internationalist Publishing Company

96 Walter Street/ Suite 200

Boston, MA 02131, USA

Tel: 617-354-7722

www.internationalist.com

PN@internationalist.com

The Internationalist is a Registered Trademark. "Key Facts" and "The Internationalist Business Guides" are Trademarks of The Internationalist Publishing Company.

All Rights are reserved under International, Pan-American, and Pan-Asian Conventions. No part of this book may be reproduced in any form without the written permission of the publisher. All rights vigorously enforced

Table Of Contents

Chapter 1: Background

Chapter 2: Geography

Chapter 3: People and Society

Chapter 4: Government and Key Leaders

Chapter 5: Economy

Chapter 6: Energy

Chapter 7: Communications

Chapter 8: Transportation

Chapter 9: Military

Chapter 10: Transnational Issues

Map of Chile

Chapter 1: Background

Prior to the arrival of the Spanish in the 16th century, the Inca ruled northern Chile while the Mapuche inhabited central and southern Chile. Although Chile declared its independence in 1810, decisive victory over the Spanish was not achieved until 1818. In the War of the Pacific (1879-83), Chile defeated Peru and Bolivia and won its present northern regions. It was not until the 1880s that the Mapuche were brought under central government control. After a series of elected governments, the three-year-old Marxist government of Salvador ALLENDE was overthrown in 1973 by a military coup led by Augusto PINOCHET, who ruled until a freely elected president was inaugurated in 1990. Sound economic policies, maintained consistently since the 1980s, have contributed to steady growth, reduced poverty rates by over half, and have helped secure the country's commitment to democratic and representative government. Chile has increasingly assumed regional and international leadership roles befitting its status as a stable, democratic nation.

Chapter 2: Geography

Location:

Southern South America, bordering the South Pacific Ocean, between Argentina and Peru

Geographic coordinates:

Southern South America, bordering the South Pacific Ocean, between Argentina and Peru

Map references:

South America

Area:

total: 756,102 sq km

country comparison to the world: 38

land: 743,812 sq km

water: 12,290 sq km

Area - comparative:

slightly smaller than twice the size of Montana

Land boundaries:

total: 6,339 km

border countries: Argentina 5,308 km, Bolivia 860 km, Peru 171 km

Coastline:

6,435 km

Maritime claims:
> territorial sea: 12 nm
>
> continental shelf: 24 nm

Climate:
> temperate; desert in north; Mediterranean in central region; cool and damp in south

Terrain:
> low coastal mountains; fertile central valley; rugged Andes in east

Elevation extremes:
> lowest point: Pacific Ocean 0 m
>
> highest point: Nevado Ojos del Salado 6,880 m

Natural resources:
> copper, timber, iron ore, nitrates, precious metals, molybdenum, hydropower

Land use:
> arable land: 1.74%
>
> permanent crops: 0.6%
>
> other: 97.65% (2011)

Irrigated land:
> 11,990 sq km (2003)

Total renewable water resources:
> 922 cu km (2011)

Freshwater withdrawal (domestic/industrial/agricultural):
   total: 26.67 cu km/yr (4%/10%/86%)

   per capita: 1,603 cu m/yr (2007)

Natural hazards:
   severe earthquakes; active volcanism; tsunamis
   volcanism:
   significant volcanic activity due to more than three-dozen active volcanoes along the Andes Mountains; Lascar (elev. 5,592 m), which last erupted in 2007, is the most active volcano in the northern Chilean Andes; Llaima (elev. 3,125 m) in central Chile, which last erupted in 2009, is another of the country's most active; Chaiten's 2008 eruption forced major evacuations; other notable historically active volcanoes include Cerro Hudson, Copahue, Guallatiri, Llullaillaco, Nevados de Chillan, Puyehue, San Pedro, and Villarrica

Environment - current issues:
   widespread deforestation and mining threaten natural resources; air pollution from industrial and vehicle emissions; water pollution from raw sewage

Environment - international agreements:
   party to: Antarctic-Environmental Protocol, Antarctic-Marine Living Resources, Antarctic Seals, Antarctic Treaty, Biodiversity, Climate Change, Climate Change-Kyoto Protocol, Desertification, Endangered Species, Environmental Modification, Hazardous Wastes, Law of the Sea, Marine Dumping,

Ozone Layer Protection, Ship Pollution, Wetlands, Whaling

signed, but not ratified: none of the selected agreements

Geography - note:

the longest north-south trending country in the world, extending across 38 degrees of latitude; strategic location relative to sea lanes between the Atlantic and Pacific Oceans (Strait of Magellan, Beagle Channel, Drake Passage); Atacama Desert - the driest desert in the world - spreads across the northern part of the country; the crater lake of Ojos del Salado is the world's highest lake (at 6,390 m)

Chapter 3: People and Society

Nationality:
    noun: Chilean(s)
    adjective: Chilean

Ethnic groups:
    white and white-Amerindian 95.4%, Mapuche 4%, other indigenous groups 0.6% (2002 census)

Languages:
    Spanish (official), Mapudungun, German, English

Religions:
    Roman Catholic 70%, Evangelical 15.1%, Jehovah's Witnesses 1.1%, other Christian 1%, other 4.6%, none 8.3% (2002 census)

Population:
    17,216,945 (July 2013 est.)
    country comparison to the world: 63

Age structure:
    0-14 years: 21% (male 1,846,433/female 1,771,225)
    15-24 years: 16.6% (male 1,457,772/female 1,398,684)
    25-54 years: 43.2% (male 3,694,178/female 3,738,355)
    55-64 years: 9.6% (male 771,790/female 872,824)
    65 years and over: 9.7% (male 694,570/female 971,114)
    (2013 est.)

Median age:
> total: 33 years
> male: 31.8 years
> female: 34.3 years (2013 est.)

Population growth rate:
> 0.86% (2013 est.)
> country comparison to the world: 128

Birth rate:
> 14.12 births/1,000 population (2013 est.)
> country comparison to the world: 143

Death rate:
> 5.86 deaths/1,000 population (2013 est.)
> country comparison to the world: 172

Net migration rate:
> 0.35 migrant(s)/1,000 population (2013 est.)
> country comparison to the world: 71

Urbanization:
> urban population: 89% of total population (2010)
> rate of urbanization: 1.1% annual rate of change (2010-15 est.)

Major urban areas - population:
> SANTIAGO (capital) 6.034 million; Valparaiso 865,000 (2011)

Sex ratio:

at birth: 1.04 male(s)/female

0-14 years: 1.04 male(s)/female

15-24 years: 1.04 male(s)/female

25-54 years: 0.99 male(s)/female

55-64 years: 0.88 male(s)/female

65 years and over: 0.71 male(s)/female

total population: 0.97 male(s)/female (2013 est.)

Maternal mortality rate:

25 deaths/100,000 live births (2010)

country comparison to the world: 132

Infant mortality rate:

total: 7.19 deaths/1,000 live births

country comparison to the world: 160

male: 7.67 deaths/1,000 live births

female: 6.68 deaths/1,000 live births (2013 est.)

Life expectancy at birth:

total population: 78.27 years

country comparison to the world: 53

male: 75.25 years

female: 81.42 years (2013 est.)

Total fertility rate:

1.85 children born/woman (2013 est.)

country comparison to the world: 148

Health expenditures:
>7.5% of GDP (2011)
>
>country comparison to the world: 74

Physicians density:
>1.03 physicians/1,000 population (2009)

Hospital bed density:
>2 beds/1,000 population (2010)

Drinking water source:
>improved:
>>*urban*: 99.5% of population
>>
>>*rural*: 90.1% of population
>>
>>*total*: 98.5% of population
>
>unimproved:
>>*urban*: 0.5% of population
>>
>>*rural*: 9.9% of population
>>
>>*total*: 1.5% of population (2011 est.)

Sanitation facility access:
>improved:
>>*urban*: 99.8% of population
>>
>>*rural*: 89.4% of population
>>
>>*total*: 98.7% of population

unimproved:
- *urban*: 0.2% of population
- *rural*: 10.6% of population
- *total*: 1.3% of population (2011 est.)

HIV/AIDS - adult prevalence rate:

0.4% (2009 est.)

country comparison to the world: 71

HIV/AIDS - people living with HIV/AIDS:

40,000 (2009 est.)

country comparison to the world: 61

HIV/AIDS - deaths:

NA

Obesity - adult prevalence rate:

29.4% (2008)

country comparison to the world: 30

Education expenditures:

4.2% of GDP (2010)

country comparison to the world: 104

Literacy:

definition: age 15 and over can read and write

total population: 98.6%

male: 98.6%

female: 98.5% (2009 est.)

School life expectancy (primary to tertiary education):
  total: 15 years
  male: 15 years
  female: 15 years (2011)
Unemployment, youth ages 15-24:
  total: 17.5%
  country comparison to the world: 73

Chapter 4: Government and Key Leaders

Country name:

    conventional long form: Republic of Chile

    conventional short form: Chile

    local long form: Republica de Chile

    local short form: Chile

Government type:

    republic

Capital:

    name: Santiago

    geographic coordinates: 33 27 S, 70 40 W

    time difference: UTC-4 (1 hour ahead of Washington, DC during Standard Time)

Administrative divisions:

    15 regions (regiones, singular - region); Aysen, Antofagasta, Araucania, Arica y Parinacota, Atacama, Biobio, Coquimbo, Libertador General Bernardo O'Higgins, Los Lagos, Los Rios, Magallanes y de la Antartica Chilena, Maule, Region Metropolitana (Santiago), Tarapaca, Valparaiso

Independence:

    18 September 1810 (from Spain)

National holiday:

    Independence Day, 18 September (1810)

Constitution:
>many previous; latest adopted 11 September 1980, effective 11 March 1981; amended many times, last in 2011 (2011)

Legal system:
>civil law system influenced by several West European civil legal systems; judicial review of legislative acts by the Constitutional Tribunal

International law organization participation:
>has not submitted an ICJ jurisdiction declaration; accepts ICCt jurisdiction

Suffrage:
>18 years of age; universal and voluntary

Executive branch:
>chief of state: President Sebastian PINERA Echenique (since 11 March 2010); note - the president is both the chief of state and head of government
>
>head of government: President Sebastian PINERA Echenique (since 11 March 2010)
>
>cabinet: Cabinet appointed by the president
>
>elections: president elected by popular vote for a single four-year term; election last held on 17 November 2013 with a runoff election held on 15 December 2013 (next to be held 19 November 2017)

election results: Michelle BACHELET Jeria elected president; percent of vote - Michelle BACHELET Jeria 62.2%; Evelyn Rose MATTHEI Fornet 37.8%; note - BACHELET is expected to take office 11 March 2014

Legislative branch:

bicameral National Congress or Congreso Nacional consists of the Senate or Senado (38 seats; members elected by popular vote to serve eight-year terms; one-half elected every four years) and the Chamber of Deputies or Camara de Diputados (120 seats; members are elected by popular vote to serve four-year terms)

elections: Senate - last held on 13 December 2009 (next to be held in November 2013); Chamber of Deputies - last held on 13 December 2009 (next to be held in November 2013)

election resultsSenate - percent of vote by party - NA; seats by party - CPD 9 (PDC 4, PPD 3, PS 2), APC 9 (RN 6, UDI 3); Chamber of Deputies - percent of vote by party - NA; seats by party - APC 58 (UDI 37, RN 18, other 3), CPD 57 (PDC 19, PPD 18, PS 11, PRSD 5, PC 3, other 1), PRI 3, independent 2; note - as of 19 February 2013, the composition of the entire legislature is as follows: Senate - seats by party - CPD 19 (PDC 9, PPD 4, PS 5, PRSD 1), Coalition for Change (former APC) 16 (RN 8, UDI 8), independent 2, MAS 1; Chamber of Deputies - seats by party - Coalition for Change (former APC) 56 (UDI 39,

RN 17), CPD 53 (PDC 19, PPD 18, PS 11, PRSD 5), independent 5, PC 3, PRI 2, IC 1

Judicial branch:

Highest court(s): Supreme Court or Corte Suprema (consists of a court president and 20 members or ministros); Constitutional Court (consists of 7 members); Electoral Court (consists of 5 members)

Judge selection and term of offfice: Supreme Court judges appointed by the president and ratified by the Senate from lists of candidates provided by the court itself; judges appointed for life with mandatory retirement at age 70; Constitutional Court members appointed - 3 by the Supreme Court, 1 by the president of the republic, 2 by the National Security Council, and 1 by the Senate; members serve 8-year terms with partial court replacement every 4 years (the court reviews constitutionality of legislation); Electoral Court member appointments - 4 by the Supreme Court and 1 a former president or vice-president of the Senate or Chamber of Deputies selected by the Supreme Court; member term NA

subordinate courts: Courts of Appeal; oral criminal tribunals; military tribunals; local police courts; specialized tribunals and courts in matters such as family, labor, customs, taxes, and electoral affairs

Political parties and leaders:

Broad Social Movement or MAS [Alejandro NAVARRO Brain]
Citizen Left or IC
Equality Party [Lautaro GUANCA Vallejos]
Coalition for Change or CC (also known as the Alliance for Chile (Alianza) or APC) (including National Renewal or RN [Carlos LARRAIN Pena], and Independent Democratic Union or UDI [Patricio MELERO]
Coalition of Parties for Democracy (Concertacion) or CPD (including Christian Democratic Party or PDC [Ignacio WALKER Prieto], Party for Democracy or PPD [Jaime Daniel QUINTANA Leal], Radical Social Democratic Party or PRSD [Jose Antonio GOMEZ Urrutia], and Socialist Party or PS [Osvaldo ANDRADE Lara])
Communist Party of Chile (Partido Comunista de Chile) or PC [Guillermo TEILLIER del Valle]
Ecological Green Party [Cristian VILLAROEL Novoa]
Humanist Party or PH [Danilo MONTEVERDE Reyes]
Independent Regionalist Party or PRI [Carlos OLIVARES Zepeda]
Progressive Party or PRO [Marco ENRIQUEZ-OMINAMI Gumucio]

Political pressure groups and leaders:

Roman Catholic Church, particularly conservative groups such as Opus Dei
United Labor Central or CUT includes trade unionists from the country's five largest labor confederations
other: university student federations at all major universities

International organization participation:
APEC, BIS, BRICS, CAN (associate), CD, CELAC, FAO, G-15, G-77, IADB, IAEA, IBRD, ICAO, ICC (national committees), ICRM, IDA, IFAD, IFC, IFRCS, IHO, ILO, IMF, IMO, IMSO, Interpol, IOC, IOM, IPU, ISO, ITSO, ITU, ITUC (NGOs), LAES, LAIA, Mercosur (associate), MIGA, MINUSTAH, NAM, OAS, OECD (Enhanced Engagement, OPANAL, OPCW, PCA, SICA (observer), UN, UNASUR, UNCTAD, UNESCO, UNFICYP, UNHCR, UNIDO, Union Latina, UNMOGIP, UNTSO, UNWTO, UPU, WCO, WFTU (NGOs), WHO, WIPO, WMO, WTO

Diplomatic representation in the US:
chief of mission: Ambassador Felipe BULNES Serrano (since 5 April 2012)
telephone: [1] (202) 785-1746
Consulate(s) general: Chicago, Los Angeles, Miami, New York, Philadelphia, San Francisco

Diplomatic representation from the US:
chief of mission: Ambassador (vacant); Charge d'Affaires Stephen M. LISTON
embassy: Avenida Andres Bello 2800, Las Condes, Santiago
mailing address: APO AA 34033
telephone: [56] (2) 330-3000

FAX: [56] (2) 330-3710, 330-3160

Key Leaders:

- Pres. — Sebastian PINERA Echenique
- Min. of Agriculture — Luis MAYOL Bouchon
- Min. of Communications & the Press — Cecilia PEREZ Jara
- Min. of Economy, Development, & Tourism — Felix DE VICENTE Mingo
- Min. of Education — Carolina SCHMIDT Zaldivar
- Min. of Energy — Jorge BUNSTER Betteley
- Min. for the Environment — Maria Ignacia BENITEZ Pereira
- Min. of Finance — Felipe LARRAIN Bascunan
- Min. of Foreign Affairs — Alfredo MORENO Charme
- Min. of Health — Jaime MANALICH Muxi
- Min. of Housing, Urban Development, & National Patrimony — Rodrigo PEREZ Mackenna
- Min. of Interior & Public Security — Andres CHADWICK
- Min. of Justice — Patricia PEREZ Goldberg
- Min. of Labor & Social Security — Juan Carlos JOBET
- Min. of Mining — Hernan DE SOLMINIHAC Tampier
- Min. of the National Council for Culture & the Arts — Robert AMPUERO

- Min. of National Defense — Rodrigo HINZPETER Kirberg
- Min. of the National Service for Women — Loreto SEGUEL King
- Min. of Planning & Cooperation — Bruno BARANDA
- Min. of Policy Coordination — Cristian LARROULET Vignau
- Min. of Public Works — Loreto SILVA
- Min. of Transport & Telecommunications — Pedro Pablo ERRAZURIZ Dominguez
- Pres., Central Bank — Rodrigo VERGARA Montes
- Ambassador to the US — Felipe BULNES Serrano
- Permanent Representative to the UN, New York — Octavio ERRAZURIZ Guilisasti

Flag description:

two equal horizontal bands of white (top) and red; a blue square the same height as the white band at the hoist-side end of the white band; the square bears a white five-pointed star in the center representing a guide to progress and honor; blue symbolizes the sky, white is for the snow-covered Andes, and red represents the blood spilled to achieve independence
note: design was influenced by the US flag

National symbol(s):

huemul (mountain deer); Andean condor

National anthem:

<u>name</u>: "Himno Nacional de Chile" (National Anthem of Chile)

Chapter 5: Economy

Economy - overview:

Chile has a market-oriented economy characterized by a high level of foreign trade and a reputation for strong financial institutions and sound policy that have given it the strongest sovereign bond rating in South America. Exports account for approximately one-third of GDP, with commodities making up some three-quarters of total exports. Copper alone provides 19% of government revenue. From 2003 through 2012, real growth averaged almost 5% per year, despite the slight contraction in 2009 that resulted from the global financial crisis. Chile deepened its longstanding commitment to trade liberalization with the signing of a free trade agreement with the US, which took effect on 1 January 2004. Chile has 22 trade agreements covering 60 countries including agreements with the European Union, Mercosur, China, India, South Korea, and Mexico. Chile has joined the United States and nine other countries in negotiating the Trans-Pacific-Partnership trade agreement. In 2012, foreign direct investment inflows reached $28.2 billion, an increase of 63% over the previous record set in 2011. The Chilean Government has generally followed a countercyclical fiscal policy, accumulating surpluses in sovereign wealth funds during periods of high copper prices and economic growth, and generally allowing deficit spending only during periods of low copper prices and growth. As of 31 December 2012, those sovereign wealth funds - kept mostly outside the country and separate from Central Bank reserves - amounted to more than $20.9 billion. Chile used these funds to finance fiscal stimulus packages during the 2009 economic downturn. In May 2010 Chile signed the OECD Convention, becoming the first South American country to join the OECD.

GDP (purchasing power parity):
$316.9 billion (2012 est.)
country comparison to the world: 43
$300.1 billion (2011 est.)
$283.7 billion (2010 est.)
note: data are in 2012 US dollars

GDP (official exchange rate):
$264.5 billion (2012 est.)

GDP - real growth rate:
5.6% (2012 est.)
country comparison to the world: 50
5.8% (2011 est.)
5.7% (2010 est.)

GDP - per capita (PPP):
$18,200 (2012 est.)
country comparison to the world: 72
$17,400 (2011 est.)
$16,600 (2010 est.)
note: data are in 2012 US dollars

GDP - composition by sector:
- agriculture: 3.6%
- industry: 36%
- services: 60.4% (2012 est.)

Labor force:
- 8.234 million (2012 est.)
- country comparison to the world: 59

Labor force - by occupation:
- agriculture: 13.2%
- industry: 23%
- services: 63.9% (2005)

Unemployment rate:
- 6.3% (2012 est.)
- country comparison to the world: 68
- 6.6% (2011 est.)

Population below poverty line:
- 15.1% (2009 est.)

Household income or consumption by percentage share:
- lowest 10%: 1.5%
- highest 10%: 42.8% (2009 est.)

Distribution of family income - Gini index:
- 52.1 (2009)
- country comparison to the world: 15
- 57.1 (2000)

Budget:
    revenues: $58.81 billion

    expenditures: $$57.38 billion (2012 est.)

Taxes and other revenues:
    22.2% of GDP (2012 est.)

    country comparison to the world: 153

Budget surplus (+) or deficit (-):
    0.5% of GDP (2012 est.)

    country comparison to the world: 39

Public debt:
    11.9% of GDP (2012 est.)

    country comparison to the world: 141

    11.1% of GDP (2011 est.)

Inflation rate (consumer prices):
    3% (2012 est.)

    country comparison to the world: 95

    3.3% (2011 est.)

Fiscal year:
    Calendar year

Central bank discount rate:
    3.12% (31 December 2010 est.)

    country comparison to the world: 139

    0.5% (31 December 2009 est.)

Commercial bank prime lending rate:
>10.06% (31 December 2012 est.)
>country comparison to the world: 98
>9.03% (31 December 2011 est.)

Stock of narrow money:
>$40.95 billion (31 December 2012 est.)
>country comparison to the world: 52
>$34.54 billion (31 December 2011 est.)

Stock of broad money:
>$193.2 billion (31 December 2011 est.)
>country comparison to the world: 41
>$191.7 billion (31 December 2010 est.)

Stock of domestic credit:
>$202.5 billion (31 December 2012 est.)
>country comparison to the world: 39
>$164.1 billion (31 December 2011 est.)

Market value of publicly traded shares:
>$270.3 billion (31 December 2011)
>country comparison to the world: 26
>$341.6 billion (31 December 2010)
>$209.5 billion (31 December 2009)

Current account balance:
>$-9.499 billion (2012 est.)
>country comparison to the world: 175
>$-3.281 billion (2011 est.)

Exports:
>$78.28 billion (2012 est.)
>
>country comparison to the world: 47
>
>$81.46 billion (2011 est.)

Exports - commodities:
>copper, fruit, fish products, paper and pulp, chemicals, wine

Exports - partners:
>China 23.3%, US 12.3%, Japan 10.7%, South Korea 5.8%, Brazil 5.5% (2012)

Imports:
>$74.86 billion (2012 est.)
>
>country comparison to the world: 40
>
>$70.91 billion (2011 est.)

Imports - commodities:
>petroleum and petroleum products, chemicals, electrical and telecommunications equipment, industrial machinery, vehicles, natural gas

Imports - partners:
>US 22.9%, China 18.2%, Argentina 6.6%, Brazil 6.5% (2012)

Reserves of foreign exchange and gold:
>$41.65 billion (31 December 2012 est.)
>
>country comparison to the world: 46
>
>$41.94 billion (31 December 2011 est.)

Debt - external:
>$112.7 billion (31 December 2012 est.)
>country comparison to the world: 45
>$96.24 billion (31 December 2011 est.)

Stock of direct foreign investment - at home:
>$192.8 billion (31 December 2012 est.)
>country comparison to the world: 26
>$162.5 billion (31 December 2011 est.)

Stock of direct foreign investment - abroad:
>$91.3 billion (31 December 2012 est.)
>country comparison to the world: 29
>$70.21 billion (31 December 2011 est.)

Exchange rates:

Chilean pesos (CLP) per US dollar -
486.49 (2012 est.)
483.67 (2011 est.)
510.25 (2010 est.)
560.86 (2009)
509.02 (2008)

Chapter 6: Energy

Electricity - production:
 62.86 billion kWh (2011 est.)
 country comparison to the world: 43

Electricity - consumption:
 53.93 billion kWh (2010 est.)
 country comparison to the world: 44

Electricity - exports:
 0 kWh (2012 est.)
 country comparison to the world: 178

Electricity - imports:
 734 million kWh (2011 est.)
 country comparison to the world: 67

Electricity - installed generating capacity:
 16.21 million kW (2010 est.)
 country comparison to the world: 45

Electricity - from fossil fuels:
 62% of total installed capacity (2010 est.)
 country comparison to the world: 131

Electricity - from nuclear fuels:
 0% of total installed capacity (2010 est.)
 country comparison to the world: 63

Electricity - from hydroelectric plants:

33.7% of total installed capacity (2010 est.)

country comparison to the world: 65

Electricity - from other renewable sources:

4.3% of total installed capacity (2010 est.)

country comparison to the world: 47

Crude oil - production:

17,340 bbl/day (2012 est.)
country comparison to the world: 82

Crude oil - exports:

0 bbl/day (2010 est.)

country comparison to the world: 97

Crude oil - imports:

169,700 bbl/day (2010 est.)

country comparison to the world: 35

Crude oil - proved reserves:

150 million bbl (1 January 2013 es)

country comparison to the world: 66

Refined petroleum products - production:

187,200 bbl/day (2010 est.)

country comparison to the world: 57

Refined petroleum products - consumption:

321,700 bbl/day (2011 est.)

country comparison to the world: 38

Refined petroleum products - exports:
> 13,040 bbl/day (2010 est.)
>
> country comparison to the world: 81

Refined petroleum products - imports:
> 154,100 bbl/day (2010 est.)
>
> country comparison to the world: 37

Natural gas - production:
> 1.144 billion cu m (2012 est.)
>
> country comparison to the world: 63

Natural gas - consumption:
> 5.296 billion cu m (2010 est.)
>
> country comparison to the world: 59

Natural gas - exports:
> 0 cu m (2011 est.)
>
> country comparison to the world: 79

Natural gas - imports:
> 3.83 billion cu m (2012 est.)
>
> country comparison to the world: 38

Natural gas - proved reserves:
> 97.97 billion cu m (1 January 2013 es)
>
> country comparison to the world: 55

Carbon dioxide emissions from consumption of energy:
> 80.1 million Mt (2011 est.)
>
> country comparison to the world: 46

Chapter 7: Communications

Telephones - main lines in use:
>3.276 million (2012)
>country comparison to the world: 48

Telephones - mobile cellular:
>24.13 million (2012)
>country comparison to the world: 44

Telephone system:
>general assessment: privatization began in 1988; most advanced telecommunications infrastructure in South America; modern system based on extensive microwave radio relay facilities; domestic satellite system with 3 earth stations
>
>domestic: number of fixed-line connections have stagnated in recent years as mobile-cellular usage continues to increase, reaching 130 telephones per 100 persons
>
>international: country code - 56; landing points for the Pan American, South America-1, and South American Crossing/Latin America Nautilus submarine cables providing links to the US and to Central and South America; satellite earth stations - 2 Intelsat (Atlantic Ocean) (2011)

Broadcast media:

national and local terrestrial TV channels, coupled with extensive cable TV networks; the state-owned Television Nacional de Chile (TVN) network is self financed through commercial advertising revenues and is not under direct government control; large number of privately owned TV stations; about 250 radio stations (2007)

Internet country code:

.cl

Internet hosts:

2.152 million (2012)

country comparison to the world: 38

Internet users:

7.009 million (2009)

country comparison to the world: 39

Chapter 8: Transportation

Airports:
- 481 (2013)
- country comparison to the world: 15

Airports - with paved runways:
- total: 90
- over 3,047 m: 5
- 2,438 to 3,047 m: 7
- 1,524 to 2,437 m: 23
- 914 to 1,523 m: 31
- under 914 m: 24 (2013)

Airports - with unpaved runways:
- total: 391
- 2,438 to 3,047 m: 5
- 1,524 to 2,437: 11
- 914 to 1,523 m: 16
- under 914 m: 319 (2013)

Heliports:
- 1 (2013)

Pipelines:
- gas 3,160 km; liquid petroleum gas 781 km; oil 985 km; refined products 722 km (2013)

Railways:

    total: 7,082 km

    country comparison to the world: 28

    standard gauge: 3,435 km 1.676-m gauge (850 km electrified)

    narrow gague: 3,647 km 1.000-m gauge (2008)

Roadways:

    total: 77,764 km

    country comparison to the world: 62

Merchant marine:

    total: 42

    country comparison to the world: 74

    by type: bulk carrier 13, cargo 5, chemical tanker 7, container 2, liquefied gas 1, passenger 3, passenger/cargo 2, petroleum tanker 8, roll on/roll off 1

    registered in other countries: 52 (Argentina 6, Brazil 1, Honduras 1, Isle of Man 9, Liberia 9, Panama 14, Peru 6, Singapore 6) (2010)

Ports and terminals:

    Major seaports: Coronel, Huasco, Lirquen, Puerto Ventanas, San Antonio, San Vicente, Valparaiso

Chapter 9: Military

Military branches:

Army of the Nation, Chilean Navy (Armada de Chile, includes Naval Aviation, Marine Corps, and Maritime Territory and Merchant Marine Directorate (Directemar)), Chilean Air Force (Fuerza Aerea de Chile, FACh), Carabineros Corps (Cuerpo de Carabineros) (2011)

Military service age and obligation:

18-45 years of age for voluntary male and female military service, although the right to compulsory recruitment of males 18-45 is retained; service obligation is 12 months for Army and 22 months for Navy and Air Force (2012)

Manpower available for military service:

males age 16-49: 4,324,732

females age 16-49: 4,251,954 (2010 est.)

Manpower fit for military service:

males age 16-49: 3,621,475

females age 16-49: 3,561,099 (2010 est.)

Manpower reaching militarily significant age annually:

male: 141,500

female: 135,709 (2010 est.)

Military expenditures:

2.04% of GDP (2012)

country comparison to the world: 120

Chapter 10: Transnational Issues

Disputes - international:

Chile and Peru rebuff Bolivia's reactivated claim to restore the Atacama corridor, ceded to Chile in 1884, but Chile has offered instead unrestricted but not sovereign maritime access through Chile to Bolivian natural gas; Chile rejects Peru's unilateral legislation to change its latitudinal maritime boundary with Chile to an equidistance line with a southwestern axis favoring Peru; in October 2007, Peru took its maritime complaint with Chile to the ICJ; territorial claim in Antarctica (Chilean Antarctic Territory) partially overlaps Argentine and British claims; the joint boundary commission, established by Chile and Argentina in 2001, has yet to map and demarcate the delimited boundary in the inhospitable Andean Southern Ice Field (Campo de Hielo Sur)

Illicit drugs:

transshipment country for cocaine destined for Europe and the region; some money laundering activity, especially through the Iquique Free Trade Zone; imported precursors passed on to Bolivia; domestic cocaine consumption is rising, making Chile a significant consumer of cocaine (2008)

Map of Chile

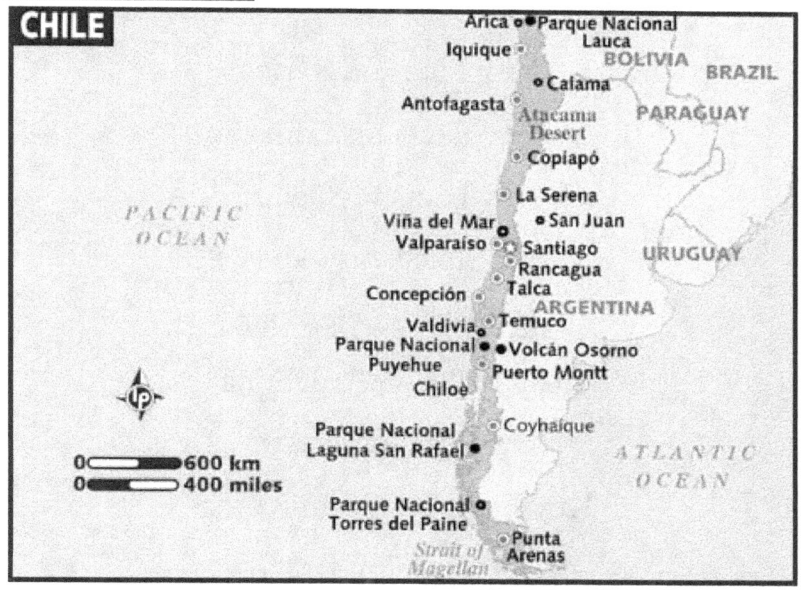

Other Key Facts™ Titles

Key Facts on Syria

Key Facts on China

Key Facts on Qatar

Key Facts on India

Key Facts on Germany

Key Facts on Argentina

Key Facts on Russia

Key Facts on North Korea

Key Facts on Brazil

Key Facts on Italy

Key Facts on the United Arab Emirates

Key Facts on the European Union

Key Facts on Pakistan

Key Facts on Saudi Arabia

Key Facts on Cyprus

Key Facts on Iran

Key Facts on Afghanistan

Key Facts on Iraq

Key Facts on Indonesia

Key Facts on South Korea

Key Facts on France

Key Facts on the United Kingdom

Key Facts on Egypt

Key Facts on Israel

All Key Facts™ Titles are Available at www.Amazon.com

THE INTERNATIONALIST®

2014

WWW.INTERNATIONALIST.COM

www.ingramcontent.com/pod-product-compliance
Lightning Source LLC
Chambersburg PA
CBHW070716180526
45167CB00004B/1495